One Duck

Velyn Cooper

ISBN-10: 1489512683
ISBN-13: 9781489512680

VC Productions
vcproductions1@gmail.com

Photos by Velyn Cooper
photosbyvelyn@gmail.com

Welcome

One duck sits on the ground.

He gets hungry
and looks for food
in the grass.

He finds a little bit of food but that is not enough, so he looks for more.

Then he sees his food bin.
He goes over and starts to eat.

Hmm! Hmm! The food is so good.

After eating, he cleans himself.

Then he goes looking for fun things to do.

He takes a walk in the grass. That is not fun.

He stands on a piece of
wood. That is not fun.

He is still hungry so he goes looking for more food.

He does not find anymore food so he goes looking for some friends to play with.

He finds one of his friends. Now there are two ducks.

He looks again and
finds one more friend.
Now there are
three ducks.

The three ducks have fun by the water.

Then they all walk home.

Other Children's Books by Velyn Cooper

Curly Tail
Curly Tail and The Sun
Rusty the Rat
Two Ducks
Let's Have Fun with Music (soon to be released)

Other books by Velyn Cooper

Biblical Journeys: Passages Through Time and Into Eternity

Expressions of Love

Happy Mother's Day

High School Girls- Build A Strong Foundation & Face Your
                Future Prepared & Courageous

High School Girls- Build A Strong Foundation & Face Your
                Future Prepared & Courageous

Look to God in Faith

My Redeemer Lives – Photo Essay

Natural Arrangements – Unity in the Midst of Diversity

Poetry From the Heart

Reflections: A 90-Day Devotional

Renewing Your Mind — Transformation is a Lifelong Process

Shades of Pink – in Memory of Hartlyn Cooper Martin

The Beauty of Freeport, Grand Bahama, Bahamas

The Journey to Becoming a True Woman of Virtue

Thoughts: A Book of Quotes

Transitioning High School and Beyond —The Journey Begins

Understanding God Through Repentance, Confession and Baptism, Salvation

What Does The Bible Say About…?

If you would like to contact the author, please send your questions or comments to:

Velyn Cooper

P. O. Box F42524

Freeport, Grand Bahama

Bahamas

Email: **biblicaljourneys@gmail.com**

Website: biblicaljourneys.net

Be sure and check out our Kids Corner

http://www.biblicaljourneys.net/jabez-world-changers.html

www.ingramcontent.com/pod-product-compliance
Lightning Source LLC
Chambersburg PA
CBHW060812290526
45792CB00005BA/1621